MAKERSPACE SURVIVAL

MAKE IT OUT ALIVE

IN A

DESERT

Claudia Martin

PowerKiDS press.

New York

Published in 2018 by The Rosen Publishing Group
29 East 21st Street, New York, NY 10010

Produced for Rosen by Calcium
Editors: Sarah Eason and Jennifer Sanderson
Designer: Emma DeBanks
Picture Research: Rachel Blount
Illustrator: Venetia Dean

Picture credits: Cover: Shutterstock: Ekaterina Pokrovsky (bg), Aleksey Stemmer (br). Inside: Shutterstock:
Max Allen 7, Bumihills 22, Cdrin 24, Angel DiBilio 34, James Michael Dorse7 8, Andrey Eremin 5cr, Bill
Florence 27, HandmadePictures 15r, Mark Hilton 28, Chris Ison 18, Matt Jeppson 35, Vladislav T. Jirousek 21,
Randy Judkins 16, Mohd KhairilX 5tr, Krungchingpixs 17, Laborant 36, Seth LaGrange 13, Maxine Livingston
26, Mario.bono 11, Clari Massimiliano 33, Mieszko9 14–15, Nebojsa S 38, Ongala 41c, Alexander Panyshkin
42, Paulista 20, Vadim Petrakov 30, Maxim Petrichuk 4, 47, Quick Shot 9, Ranglen 28, Richard_lightscapes
40–41, Laurin Rinder 39, Scharfsinn 12, Sinitar 23, Sumikophoto 32, Tomis 37, VanHart 6, Vixit 44;
Wikimedia Commons: Tent86 10.

Cataloging-in-Publication Data
Names: Martin, Claudia.
Title: Make it out alive in a desert / Claudia Martin.
Description: New York : PowerKids Press, 2018. | Series: Makerspace survival | Includes index.
Identifiers: ISBN 9781499434736 (pbk.) | ISBN 9781499434675 (library bound) | ISBN 9781499434552 (6
pack)
Subjects: LCSH: Desert survival--Juvenile literature.
Classification: LCC GV200.5 M35 2018 | DDC 613.6'9--dc23

Manufactured in China.

CPSIA Compliance Information: Batch BS17PK: For Further Information contact Rosen Publishing, New York, New York at 1-800-237-9932

Please note that the publisher
does not suggest readers carry
out any practical application of
the Can You Make It? activities
and any other survival
activities in this book.

A note about measurements:
Measurements are given in U.S.
form with metric in parentheses.
The metric conversion is
rounded to make it easier to
measure.

CONTENTS

CHAPTER 1
SURVIVE
THE DESERT

You are about to be parachuted into the center of one of the world's hottest deserts. Your challenge is to make your way back to civilization beneath the burning sun. To make your mission even more difficult, you cannot bring any water, food, tents, fire starters, or cooking equipment. How will you survive?

Will You Make It Out Alive?

You can dress in your choice of clothes and footwear. You can also carry some essential equipment, such as a pocketknife, a tube of sunscreen, and sunglasses. Apart from these items, you will have to provide yourself with water, food, and shelter by making your own tools and equipment. You can use any local materials you find in the desert, as well as any recyclable man-made items you can find lying around. You will also be provided with a backpack in which you will find some useful materials and tools.

Many lizards can survive the extreme desert climate. Can you do the same?

What Is in Your Backpack?

The following materials and tools are in your backpack. When you come across a "Can You Make It?" activity in this book, you must choose from this list of items to construct it. Each item can be used only once. Study the list carefully before you set off. You can find the correct solutions for all the activities on page 45 of this book.

Can You Make It?

Materials

- 2 D batteries
- 2.2 volt light bulb
- 10 tent poles, each 6 feet (183 cm) long
- Aluminum foil
- Black construction paper
- Bucket
- Canvas tarp
- Cardboard tube
- Cord
- Electrical tape
- Electrical wire, 5 inches (13 cm) long, with the plastic coating stripped from each end
- Newspaper
- Pizza box
- Plastic wrap
- Clear plastic sheet

Tools

- Craft knife
- Pair of scissors

Cord

Craft knife

Survival Tip

Use the Internet to look up all the items in your backpack before you begin your journey. Make sure that you understand what they are and how you might be able to use them.

WORLD OF DESERTS

Before your mission begins, take a few moments to understand the hazards you will face. A desert is a region that is very dry because, on average, fewer than 10 inches (25 cm) of precipitation falls there in a year, either as rain or snow.

Great Deserts

You are going to be dropped into a hot desert, but deserts may be hot or cold, depending on their distance from the equator. Many deserts lie in two bands called the "horse latitudes" about 2,000 miles (3,200 km) north or south of the equator. Hot, moist air rises at the equator, cooling as it does. Cool air can hold less moisture than warm air, so the moisture condenses into clouds and falls as rain. The dry air spreads out before sinking, causing bands where little rain falls.

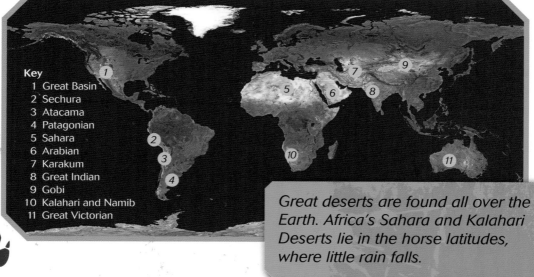

Key
1. Great Basin
2. Sechura
3. Atacama
4. Patagonian
5. Sahara
6. Arabian
7. Karakum
8. Great Indian
9. Gobi
10. Kalahari and Namib
11. Great Victorian

Great deserts are found all over the Earth. Africa's Sahara and Kalahari Deserts lie in the horse latitudes, where little rain falls.

Some deserts, such as the Mojave in the United States, form in the **rain shadow** of mountains. Warm, moist air is forced to rise over the mountains. Rain falls on the mountains, and dry air sinks on the other side. Deserts such as Asia's Gobi form in the center of huge landmasses, far from the main source of moisture: the sea.

Life in the Desert

Lack of rain means that few plants grow in the desert. The plants that can survive, such as hardy shrubs and cactuses, are able to **conserve** water. Unprotected by plants, the land is eroded, or worn away, by the wind and any water that does flow. The ground may be bare rock, gravelly, or sandy. In sandy deserts, the wind can blow the sand into mounds called **dunes**. Although daytime temperatures soar in a hot desert, on winter nights, the temperature can drop down to freezing. Desert animals are **adapted** to cope with the lack of water and extreme temperatures.

The desert-living kit fox sleeps in the cool of its underground den during the day, emerging to hunt in the evening. Could you use a similar strategy?

DESERT
PEOPLES

Deserts are **hostile** to life, so you will find very few permanent human **settlements**. However, some peoples, such as the Tuareg of the Sahara, make the desert their home. Before setting off, pick up some tips from the maker skills of the Tuareg.

Tuareg Tents

The traditional Tuareg people are nomadic, which means they travel from place to place rather than build a permanent home. Some Tuareg herd goats and sheep, moving between **seasonal** grazing areas near water sources. Some are traders, who travel across the desert on camels loaded with goods. The Tuareg sleep and shelter from the sun in tents made from stitched-together goat leather or **linen**. The frame is made of wooden posts and bars. Tents usually open along one side to keep them airy. The fire is positioned on this side for cooking, light, and heat when it becomes cold at night.

This Tuareg tent has a wind barrier outside. It is made from mats strung on poles.

Suitable Clothing

When choosing what clothing to wear for your mission, take a look at Tuareg clothes. Men wear a turban called a tagelmust. This is wound around the head, revealing only the eyes. A tagelmust protects the wearer's head from the sun and keeps windblown dust and sand out of his nose and mouth.

Both men and women wear cotton robes. These are loose-fitting, so they allow air to circulate and cool the wearer. Cotton **fibers** are made from the fluffy seed cases of the cotton plant. Cotton cloth is lightweight and allows body heat to pass through it, while **absorbing** sweat. Robes can be tied up to hold objects or to keep them out of the way of spiky acacia bushes. Acacia wood is used for firewood, and the bark fiber is wound into ropes.

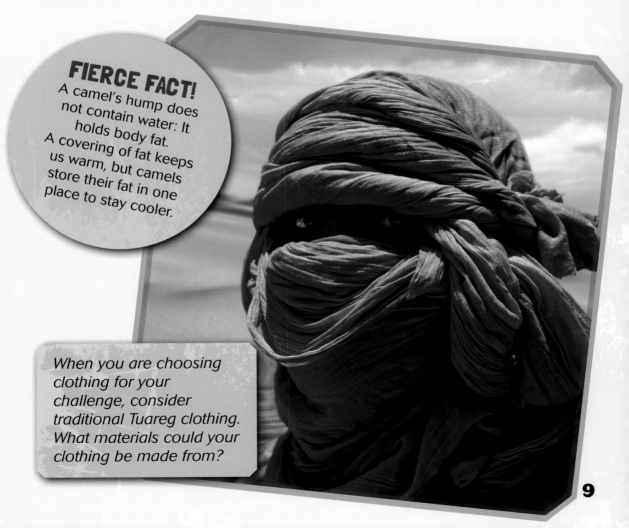

FIERCE FACT!
A camel's hump does not contain water: It holds body fat. A covering of fat keeps us warm, but camels store their fat in one place to stay cooler.

When you are choosing clothing for your challenge, consider traditional Tuareg clothing. What materials could your clothing be made from?

DESERT SURVIVOR

In 1994, Mauro Prosperi was running in the Marathon des Sables. This is a 155-mile (250 km) race through the Sahara. When a sandstorm blew up, Mauro got lost. Over the next 10 days, his maker and survival kills were put to the toughest test.

Face Protection

When the sandstorm struck, Mauro wrapped a scarf around his face and turned his back to the wind to protect his nose, eyes, and mouth. When the storm died down, the dunes had moved around, and there was no sign anywhere of Mauro's fellow runners. He set off in what he thought was the right direction, but he had guessed incorrectly.

This Marathon des Sables runner is protecting his face from the sand and sun.

665

233

If you are lost, make your way to an oasis, where you may find a settlement.

Sun Shelter

When Mauro realized that no help was arriving, he remembered some Tuareg advice: If you are lost, head in the direction of the clouds you see on the horizon early in the morning. They form from water **evaporating** from an **oasis**, where you may find other people. Set your compass for that direction, before the clouds disappear in the heat of the day.

Mauro traveled in the cool of the evenings and early mornings. He rested in the shade during the day to save energy and conserve his water. Every day, Mauro built himself a shelter from the sun using his backpack, spare clothes, and heaped-up sand. During the cooler nights, he wore a baseball cap with a woolen hat perched on top to trap his body heat.

As Mauro walked, he caught lizards and snakes to eat and sucked on the moisture of plants he found in dried riverbeds. Eventually, Mauro reached an oasis, where he sipped the water slowly, so that he did not make his parched body sick. Nearby, he found a Tuareg family, who sent for help.

FIERCE FACT!
The world's tallest sand dune is the Duna Federico Kirbus in Argentina. It is 4,035 feet (1,230 m). The region is in the rain shadow of the Andes Mountains.

CHAPTER 2
WATER, WATER

Your challenge has begun. You find yourself on the scorching desert sand, miles from the nearest settlement or road. The greatest danger that you face is dehydration, which is caused by losing more water from your body than you drink.

Know the Signs of Dehydration

Water makes up two-thirds of the human body, and without enough water, the body stops functioning properly. We lose water from our body in sweat, pee, feces, and when we breathe out.

Dehydration can sneak up on you quickly. Early signs of dehydration are a dry mouth, thirstiness, and light-headedness. You will pee less frequently, and your pee will have a dark color and strong smell. Severe dehydration causes exhaustion, confusion, dizziness, and if untreated, death.

No sensible hiker would enter a desert without plenty of water and an excellent knowledge of the area.

Stay Alive

On an ordinary day, you should drink six to eight glasses of water. In the desert, you will need to drink up to four times as much. This is because you will be sweating heavily in the scorching heat. You will sweat even more if you move around during daylight hours.

To have any chance of surviving your challenge, you need to find water immediately. This is no easy task. While you look for it, keep your mouth shut! Breathe through your nose instead. When you do find water, sip it steadily over a number of hours rather than gulping it down all at once. If you gulp it down, you will upset the balance of water and salt in your body.

The Texas horned lizard conserves water by having a very thick skin that does not let water out. It lives in the Sonoran Desert.

DIG A HOLE

The desert may look as dry as a bone, but if you follow the clues given by plants and animals, they will lead you to a water source, such as a spring, stream, or oasis. Can you see a mosquito? If you can, you are in luck!

Follow the Animals

What animals can you see? Bees will not stray farther than 2 miles (3 km) from water. Mosquitoes are found within 0.3 miles (0.5 km) of a water source. If you can see a frog, water is very close. Follow the trails of animal footprints and droppings. If several trails go in one direction, they are probably leading to water.

If you cannot find surface water, you will have to dig for it. Wherever you see a cluster of green plants, such as in a dried-out riverbed, there is likely to be water underground. Water may also soak into the ground at the bottom of cliffs after heavy rain. Use a stick to loosen the ground, then a flat stone for scraping it away. Dig until water fills the hole. To create a filter to keep sand and soil out of your water, line the hole with stones, fitting them together like a jigsaw puzzle. Empty the water the first few times the hole fills, as it will be too dirty to drink.

For thousands of years, people have dug wells to reach water that has soaked into the ground.

Purify Your Water

Water from underground may be fairly free from **parasites** and **bacteria**, but to be safe you should purify it. In the desert, you can use the sun, as the **ultraviolet light** in its rays kills germs. If you can find a clear plastic bottle, fill it with water and leave it in sunlight for six hours. In cloudy weather, this method will take two days.

A plastic bottle can be turned into a life-saving water purifier.

FIERCE FACT!
The Atacama Desert is between the Andes and the Chilean Coast mountains. It lies in a double rain shadow. Some weather stations there have never measured rain.

BAG
A PLANT

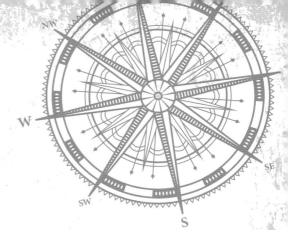

Plants release about 10 percent of the moisture in the air. They release it from their leaves, stems, and flowers. This process is called transpiration. Can you think of a way to collect that water for drinking?

Plants and Water

Plants take in water through their roots. The water travels through the plant to every leaf and bud. A plant uses up only a small amount of the water it takes in, for growing and making energy. The rest is released from tiny holes, called stomata, in the leaves and stems. The water evaporates from the stomata, changing to a gas called **water vapor** and mixing with the air. Your task is to catch that water vapor.

Plants need water to survive, like humans and all other animals.

Collecting Water

Look for a green plant that is large and healthy. Make sure it is not poisonous. Use a large, clear, clean plastic bag to allow the sun's rays to penetrate. Without damaging the plant, put the bag over a branch, then tie it gently but securely, so that no air can get out. Over the course of a sunny day, a large branch may release as much as 4 cups (1 l) of water.

The plant's stomata release the water as water vapor. When the water vapor touches the plastic, it cools and condenses into liquid water. If you build your water catcher wisely, you can create a funnel at the bottom of the bag by loosely tying a string around one corner. If you had a plastic tube, you could insert it in the collection chamber to drink.

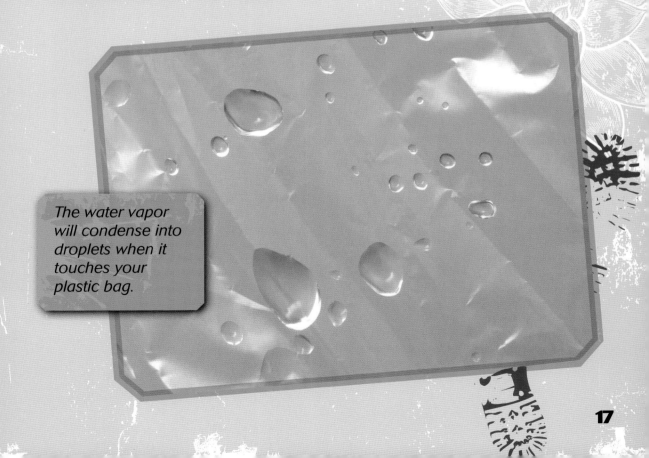

FIERCE FACT!
During one year, a large oak tree can transpire 40,000 gallons (151,000 l) of water. Unfortunately, you will not find many large trees in the desert!

The water vapor will condense into droplets when it touches your plastic bag.

USE THE SUN

On the previous pages, you learned how to use a plastic bag to collect the water that evaporates from plants. You can take the method a step further to build your own **solar** still. Solar stills use the sun's heat to collect moisture from the soil as well as plants.

Solar Still

A still is a piece of equipment that purifies water by heating it until it evaporates into water vapor, then condenses it into liquid water again. During this process, the water leaves behind many of its **impurities**, usually making it safe to drink. A solar still performs this process using the heat of the sun.

If you dig a hole in a dried-out riverbed, you will notice that the soil or sand starts to look damper the deeper you dig. The aim of your still is to capture this moisture. Eventually, the sun's heat will make the moisture evaporate into water vapor. Think about how you could trap it and condense it.

The green tree frog survives in the Australian desert by hopping from the cool outdoors to a warm tree hole. This makes condensation on the frog's skin, which it soaks up.

Make It Out Alive

Make a Solar Still

From your list of supplies and some local materials, you will need to make:

→ A hole in a damp spot, in which you can also put plants to collect the water from their transpiration
→ A cover on which water vapor will condense into liquid water
→ A container to collect the drinking water.

Can You Make It?

Step 1
You need to start by digging a hole in the ground. Where should it be positioned? What local materials could you use for digging?

Step 2
Which item could be used as a cover for your still? It will need to trap moist air and cause condensation.

Step 3
Consider which item you will use to collect the condensed water.

Step 4
What local materials could weigh down your cover so it does not blow away? How could you slightly weigh down your cover, so that the condensed water drips into your container rather than onto the ground?

Weights to hold cover in place

Cover

Weight to ensure water drips into container

Condensed water

Container for condensed water

CHAPTER 3
KEEP COOL

There is little shade in the desert. The dry air means that clouds do not often form to give you a break from the beating sun. It is vital that you understand the risks of overheating. You will need to use your maker skills to protect yourself.

Recognize Heatstroke

You will find that you get hot and tired in the desert almost instantly. If your skin is not covered, it will start to burn. After a while, you may have a headache and begin to feel sick and dizzy. This is called heat exhaustion. If you stay in the sun any longer, you will develop heatstroke. This is when your body is so hot that it cannot cool itself. You will feel confused and may collapse. If untreated, heatstroke is fatal.

The air temperature in Death Valley, in California's Mojave Desert, goes as high as 134° F (57° C), making it one of the world's hottest places.

What Should You Do?

Never walk, dig a well, climb a dune, or do any other exercise during the day. Save your exertion for the hours around dawn or just after sunset. During the day, try to set up a shade for yourself. Cover your skin in loose-fitting clothes. Wear headwear that shades your face and your neck at all times. Make sure you use the sunscreen and the sunglasses that you have brought with you, as the sun's rays can reflect off the sand and rock, producing dangerous glare.

If you start to feel unwell, move into the shade immediately, and drink water. Cool your skin using a damp cloth. Soak your head covering in water. If your skin has been burned, it may not start to redden or blister for a few hours. Get help if you possibly can.

The Cape ground squirrel uses its bushy tail as a sunshade in the Kalahari Desert. Could you make a sunshade?

FIERCE FACT!
The Loot Desert in Iran holds the record for the highest land surface temperature. The sand there can reach 159° F (71° C).

HAT ATTACK

A hat is essential to shade your head, face, and neck. What design of headwear is the best? Should you wear a tagelmust like the Tuareg or a safari helmet like an old-fashioned explorer? What material should the ideal hat be made from?

Different Choices

Traditionally, tagelmusts are dyed dark blue. Dark colors absorb more of the sun's damaging rays than light colors. So a dark T-shirt gives better protection against getting sunburned through the material than a white T-shirt made from the same fabric. However, when the dark fabric absorbs rays, it heats up, so dark fabric must be loose-fitting to be comfortable in the sun. In contrast, white fabric reflects rather than absorbs the sun's heat, so it stays cooler.

Many desert-dwellers wear a keffiyeh, *which is a loose, checked cotton scarf headdress.*

A safari helmet has the benefit of a wide brim for shade, and its raised **crown**, which is punctured with a few holes, allows air to circulate between the wearer's head and the fabric. This makes it feel cooler than a tight hat. A panama hat, woven loosely from straw, allows a lot of air to circulate.

Design Your Own

If you were designing the ideal hat for desert wear, what shape would it be? Perhaps your hat could combine the benefits of a wide brim and high crown with extra protection for the neck and face. What materials could it be made from? Consider the fact that some fabrics feel more comfortable in high temperatures than others. For example, fabrics made from plant fibers, such as cotton and linen, absorb sweat well, allowing it to evaporate. They also allow body heat to pass through them. What color would you make your hat? Maybe it could have an outer layer that is one color and an inner layer of another color.

Would you make any modifications to this hat to improve its performance?

FIERCE FACT!
Fiber from the flax plant was probably one of the first fibers to be woven into cloth, at least 25,000 years ago. Flax fibers make linen.

IN THE SHADE

In the heat of the day, your best chance of survival is to make yourself a shelter to protect yourself from the sun. At night, when the temperature drops, you will be grateful for the warmth your shelter provides.

Tepee Time

The benefit of building a **tepee** shelter is that it is self-supporting: You do not need to find a tree from which to dangle your shelter or prop it up. Traditionally, the Native Americans of the Great Plains built tepees. These tents were made from a frame of branches tied in a cone shape and covered with animal skins. Flaps could be opened at the top and front of the tepee. These would give **ventilation** during hot weather and release smoke from the central fire. Tepees were attached to the ground with wooden pegs. There is little wood in the desert to help with your build, so what materials will you use?

Without any man-made materials, a tepee can be constructed from branches and ropes made from plant fibers.

24

Make a Tepee

From your list of supplies and some local materials, you will need to make:

→ A tepee shelter with room for you to sleep inside
→ A large doorway for your shelter, which can be open during the day to keep it airy and closed during the cooler nighttime.

Can You Make It?

Step 1
Think about which items you will use to create a cone-shaped frame for your tepee.

Step 2
Which item could you use to tie your frame together?

Step 3
Which item could be used as a cover for your shelter? How and where will you attach it to the frame? What local materials could weigh down your construction?

Step 4
Think about ventilation for your tepee. Do you need to modify your design to create a doorway that can close?

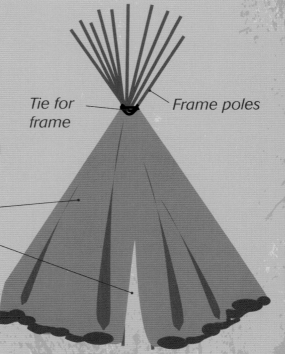

Tie for frame

Frame poles

Cover

Doorway

Materials to weigh down construction

CHAPTER 4
GET COOKING

Now that you have met your most immediate needs of finding water and shade, it is time to find something to eat. The desert may seem lifeless, but if you know where to look, there is food to be found.

Crawlers and Slitherers

People who have survived being lost in the desert all have one thing in common: They overcame their disgust when choosing what to eat. They survived by catching insects, reptiles such as lizards, and small **mammals**. You must remember that many insects and lizards are poisonous. Some people have dangerous allergies to insect stings. Most animals will give you a nasty, or even a deadly, bite.

Chasing after hopping or fluttering insects will get you nowhere in the desert. The best solution is to trap them. Many, but not all, grasshoppers are **edible**. You can make a grasshopper trap by cutting the top off a plastic bottle, putting in some overripe fruit or other bait, and half-burying it in the ground. When you catch a grasshopper, it must be cooked thoroughly. If you are not in a survival situation, let your grasshoppers go unharmed.

Poisonous grasshoppers, like the eastern lubber, can often be recognized by their bright colors. These warn predators that they can be deadly.

Prickly Snack

In the deserts of the Southwest or Mexico, a useful plant to recognize is the prickly pear cactus. Its pink fruits are tasty and packed with water, sugar, and fiber. However, you will have to twist them safely off the spine-covered cactus first. Try constructing tongs using the materials in your backpack. The fruits themselves are covered in hairs that will fix themselves in your skin like glass. Do not touch them. Using your tongs, roll the fruits in sand or grit to detach the hairs. Still without touching the fruits, peel them with your pocketknife.

FIERCE FACT!
Never hunt for food in the wild without the help of a knowledgeable guide. Never touch an unidentified animal or plant.

The fruits of the prickly pear cactus are called "tuna" in Spanish.

BURY IT

You do not have matches or a cooking pot, so how are you going to cook your food? You will have to use your maker skills and a little ingenuity. Your first task is to dig a hole in the sand.

Make a Sandpit

Dig your hole in the sand about 3 feet (91 cm) deep and 3 feet (91 cm) across. Collect plenty of dried animal feces, such as camel dung. You will be using this as fuel for your fire. Now you need to light a fire in your pit.

Collect tinder for your fire. Tinder is any dry material that will burn easily, such as shreds of leaves, twigs, or bark. Use a magnifying glass or glasses lens to concentrate the sun's rays on your tinder until the heat sets it on fire. Alternatively, use the **friction** method. Find two dry branches or strong plant stems. Strip away the bark using your pocketknife. Cut a hole or groove in one of the pieces of wood. Twist the other piece of wood in the hole, or rub it along the groove until the friction creates enough heat to make a glowing ember. When your tinder is lit, feed the fire with larger pieces of dried grass or twigs.

Camel dung can be used as fuel. It can also be mixed with straw and mud to build a shelter.

Fire Pit

Drop your camel dung into the fire pit. When the dung is glowing hot, wrap your food carefully in the leaves of a nonpoisonous plant. Place your sealed food on top of the glowing camel dung coals. Using a stick, cover your food packages with coals. Fill the hole with sand. Now you must wait: This cooking method is slow. A large animal will take many hours, but a lizard will be ready in just an hour or two.

This man is starting a fire using friction, as humans have done for thousands of years.

FIERCE FACT!
Camel dung contains the bacteria *Bacillus subtilis*, which desert people use to treat stomach infections. The bacteria is also made in laboratories.

SUNNY OVEN

In one hour, Earth receives as much energy from the sun as humans use in an entire year. The desert is a perfect place to harness the power of the sun. Use your maker skills to construct an oven that cooks food using only the sun's heat.

Solar Oven

To build your solar oven, consider the properties of different materials. You need to direct the sun's rays into your oven and then prevent the heat from escaping. Shiny metals, such as mirrors, are good at reflecting the sun's rays. On page 22, we looked at how black materials become hot as they absorb the sun's heat. On page 17, we used clear plastic to trap warm air. Finally, some materials, such as wool and paper, are good **insulators**. This means they prevent heat from escaping.

On a hot day, the temperature inside these two solar ovens may reach 200° F (93° C). This is too cool to cook meat but warm enough to slow-roast vegetables.

Make a Solar Oven

From your list of supplies and some local materials, you will need to make:

→ A well-insulated box to hold food for cooking
→ A lid for the box that can be angled to reflect the sun's rays onto the food
→ A see-through cover for the food-holding base of the oven to trap the sun's heat.

Can You Make It?

Step 1
Think about which item could form the basic frame of your oven. Will you make any cuts in this item to modify its shape?

Step 2
Which items could insulate your oven? Think about which colors are good at absorbing heat. Which materials are good insulators?

Step 3
Which item will you use to cover the inside of your lid? Which local material could be used to prop open the lid at a good angle?

Step 4
Once you have placed food inside your oven, which item could you use to wrap the section of the oven that holds food? It should be a see-through cover to trap the sun's heat.

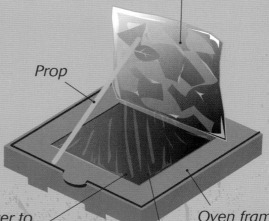

Lid cover to reflect the sun's rays onto oven

Prop

See-through cover to trap the sun's heat

Oven frame

Color for absorbing heat

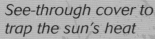

CHAPTER 5
DESERT DANGERS

As you make your way back to civilization, remember that there are many other hazards to watch out for in the desert, from sandstorms to flash floods. It is hard to believe, but more people drown in the desert than die of thirst.

Flash Floods

A flash flood is when low-lying land is flooded very quickly. Rain is infrequent in the desert, but when it does arrive, it can be torrential and accompanied by thunder and lightning. The dry, hard, rocky ground in the desert means that water is slow to soak into the earth. Instead, it flows over the surface, finding the easiest path: a riverbed or **canyon**. The lack of regular rain means that these channels may be clogged up with debris, such as rocks and fallen logs. The flood will sweep along this debris, making it even more dangerous.

A summer storm has turned this dry riverbed into a muddy torrent.

The Lay of the Land

Most people who are hurt in flash floods are taken by surprise, so be prepared. If you hear thunder or see the first raindrops, move to high ground fast. Beware of walking through narrow canyons. Always keep in mind where your escape route would be.

Even if it does not look like it will rain, never camp in a dried-out riverbed or canyon. You can spot a riverbed because there may be some signs of plant life. When choosing a place to sleep, examine the geography of the local area. Where would water flow if it had to cross this piece of land?

FIERCE FACT!
It takes only 6 inches (15 cm) of swiftly moving water to knock a walker off her feet. Just 1 foot (30 cm) of water can send a car out of control.

If the water level rose quickly, the steep sides of this canyon would prevent escape.

33

SLIDERS AND STINGERS

The most dangerous animals in the desert are those that crawl and slither across the ground. To sleep peacefully at night and protect yourself from spiders, scorpions, and snakes, build yourself a hammock or raised bed.

Bites

Rattlesnakes and coral snakes are among the most deadly snakes you might come across in the desert. Rattlesnakes are easy to recognize by the buzzing rattle on the end of their tail. Coral snakes have one of the strongest **venoms** of any North American snake. They are red with yellow and black rings. Snakes will try to avoid you if they can, so you will be bitten only if you surprise them. Be careful where you step, and avoid crevices and caves.

The western desert tarantula lives in Arizona and Mexico. It has a venomous bite and sharp hairs on its body that it can flick onto attackers.

Stings

Scorpions are common in deserts around the world. They are feared for the powerful venom they can inject with a sting from their tail. Shake out your shoes and clothes before you put them on in the morning. Do not reach into dark holes. Be careful if you are rooting through a pile of stones or firewood. If you are stung or bitten by a scorpion or snake, you will need to get antivenom fast!

Raise Yourself

To construct a raised bed, you will have to find four trees or drive four stakes into the ground to act as bedposts. Create the bed frame with four tree branches, tied with rope or wedged into place in the branches. Tie rope across your frame in a cat's cradle fashion, crisscrossing between the side branches to hold you above the ground in a net.

FIERCE FACT!
The fat-tailed scorpion of the deserts of North Africa and the Middle East is one of the world's deadliest. It kills several people every year.

The black-tailed rattlesnake lives in the deserts of the Southwest and Mexico. Rattlesnakes like to lie in the sun on rocky ledges.

SANDSTORM

Sandstorms are clouds of sand and dust picked up from the desert by strong winds. These storms can **suffocate** or **disorient** you. The grains of sand will scratch or even blind you.

Look at the Camel

When considering how best to protect yourself from sandstorms, it is worth examining the physical traits that allow camels to survive in the desert. Camels can close their nostrils to keep out sand. Their eyelashes and ear hairs are extremely long. They have an extra, see-through eyelid, called a nictitating membrane. It can be drawn across the eyeball to protect it or to dislodge grains of sand. A camel's widened feet help it to walk through sand without sinking in.

The dromedary camel of northern Africa and western Asia has a single hump.

How to Protect Yourself

In an ideal world, if you saw a sandstorm on its way, you would put on a mask that is designed to filter out dust and sand grains. Swimming goggles, combined with a scarf wrapped around your ears, nose, and mouth, would do a similar job.

As the storm closes in, try to find shelter. If there is no man-made shelter, a large rock or cliff that shields you from the force of the wind will help. However, do not seek shelter behind a sand dune, as you may be buried by it. The sand will be thickest at ground level, so if you are able to climb safely to high ground, do so. When you are in the middle of the storm, do not attempt to move through it: Stay where you are, and shield yourself from sand and larger flying objects with your backpack.

FIERCE FACT!
On average, the windy Bodélé Depression in the southern Sahara experiences sandstorms for 100 days every year.

In the thick of a sandstorm, you will not be able to see farther than a few feet ahead.

CHAPTER 6

GET OUT OF THERE

Traveling in the cool of the evening and the early mornings, it is time to find your way out of the desert. Can you spot distant green fields or a water source? That is where you may find a human settlement.

Finding the Way

Follow the example of Mauro Prosperi (see pages 10 and 11), and look for the clouds forming above oases in the early mornings. Alternatively, If you know that civilization lies to the north, set your sights on north, and keep on walking. How do you know which direction is north if you do not have a compass? If you are north of the equator, at noon—when the sun is highest in the sky—it will be due south of you. For nighttime **navigation**, learn to recognize a few star constellations. North of the equator, the North Star, also called Polaris, marks the direction of north.

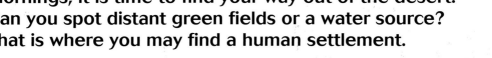

The Big Dipper, which is part of the constellation Ursa Major (the Great Bear), can point the way to Polaris, the North Star.

Polaris

Little Dipper

Draco

The Lozenge

ξ

γ

β

ν

Big Dipper

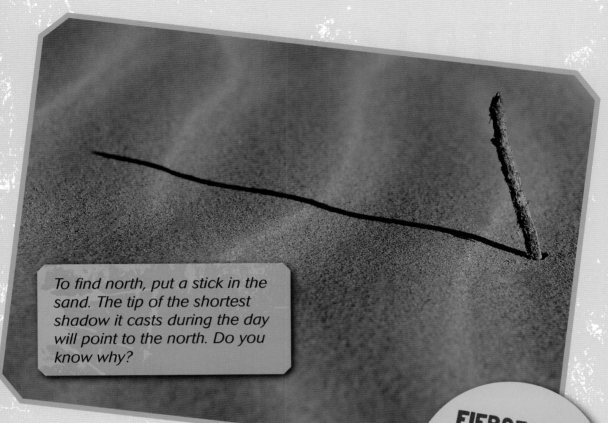

To find north, put a stick in the sand. The tip of the shortest shadow it casts during the day will point to the north. Do you know why?

Dune Directions

In the desert, an understanding of winds and how sand dunes form will help you navigate your way home. Where the sand is deep, tall sand dunes form at 90 degrees, a right angle, to the prevailing wind. The prevailing wind is the wind that is usual in a particular region. So if the prevailing wind is from the west, sand dunes form north to south. Where dunes are crescent-shaped, called barchan dunes, the horns of the crescent point in the opposite direction from the wind. In the deserts of the Southwest, the prevailing winds blow from west to southwest.

ATTRACT ATTENTION

If you are injured or unwell, the best strategy is to stay where you are and signal for help. Your signal can be something that is seen, such as a fire, or something that is heard. Think about how you can use your maker skills.

Visual Signals

At night, a fire is an ideal signal. During the day, throw green leaves on your fire to create more smoke. Adding any rubber item will create dark smoke that will be seen from a distance.

If you had a mirror, you could use it to reflect the sun's rays at a passing plane to attract attention. Are there any materials in your backpack or among your clothing that you could use to reflect light? The **SOS** signal is three short flashes, three long flashes, and three short flashes. You could also use clothes or rocks to write a signal on the ground. Make it large enough to be seen by an airplane. A "V" means "I need help."

> *Red-smoking flares were invented as a fast and safe way to send a distress signal.*

Signal Whistle

You can send out an SOS using a whistle. To make your own whistle, all you need is an empty pen casing and your pocketknife. Remove the front end of the pen, including the ink tube and the tapered section used for writing. Leave the plastic plug at the back end of the pen in place. Now cut through the remaining body of the pen, 1.5 inches (4 cm) from the back end. Cut downward onto a hard surface, and be extremely careful. Press the open end of this section to your bottom lip. Put your upper lip just above the whistle's rim, and tilt the bottom of the whistle outward. Blow across the opening.

Turn a ballpoint pen into a survival whistle.

FIERCE FACT!
Your whistle works in the same way as blowing across the top of a bottle to make a flutelike sound. Your whistle is much more high-pitched, though.

41

SHINE OUT

Traveling at night over scorpion-infested, rocky ground is dangerous. With a flashlight to illuminate your path, you would be safer, and you could signal for help. Do you have materials to make a flashlight?

Homemade Flashlight

To construct a flashlight, you need a light bulb and a source of electricity. Batteries store electrical energy. A battery has a positive and a negative **terminal**, marked "+" and "-." When two batteries are used, the negative terminal of one needs to touch the positive terminal of the other. When batteries are attached to an electrical circuit, they make electricity flow.

A circuit is a loop that electricity can flow around. It can be made from electrical wire. Inside this plastic-coated wire is copper. Copper is a metal that allows electricity to move through it. When the loop is broken, electricity will not flow. Electrical circuits become hot and should not be touched with damp hands. Never experiment with the electricity from wall plug sockets.

Send an SOS using a flashlight with three short flashes, three long flashes, and three more short flashes.

Make It Out Alive

Make a Flashlight

From your list of supplies and some local materials, you will need to make:

→ An electrical circuit containing a source of electricity and a light bulb
→ A simple switch to turn your bulb on and off
→ A container that can snugly hold your circuit.

Can You Make It?

Step 1
Think about which items will make up your electricity source. Examine them to see which way up they should be positioned.

Step 2
Which item could stick your light bulb to your electricity source?

Step 3
Consider which item will complete your circuit, running from one end of your electricity source to your light bulb. How could you make a switch to open and close the circuit? Remember, the electrical wire must touch the metal part of the light bulb to complete the electrical circuit.

Step 4
Which item could be a container for your circuit?

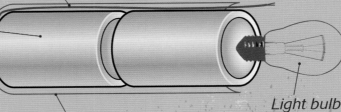

Electrical wire

Electricity source

Circuit container

Light bulb

MAKE YOUR MARK

It is easy to become disoriented in the desert and walk in circles. As you travel, mark your trail, so that you know which way you have come. This will also be a trail for rescuers to follow.

Building Cairns

Piles of stones, called **cairns**, can be used to mark your trail. Cairns are built in a rough pyramid shape, starting with the flattest stones you can find. You may be lucky enough to find a route already marked by cairns. Sometimes, the builder might have inserted a pointing stone, or beak, into the cairn to mark the direction of travel. At each cairn, look around for the next, then keep it in your line of sight.

You Survived!

At last, in the distance, you spot a line of camels. As you get closer, you see Tuareg traders are riding them. You ask if you can travel with them. One of the Tuareg orders a camel to kneel so you can climb aboard. You wrap your legs around the camel's hump as it lurches across the sand toward the nearest market.

Follow a camel caravan: Tuareg traders have been navigating the desert for hundreds of years.

ANSWERS—
DID YOU MAKE IT?

Did your makerspace survival skills pass the test? Did you select the best equipment for each "Make It Out Alive" activity? Check your choices against the answers below.

Page 19 Solar Still
Bucket • Clear plastic sheet
Dig your hole in full sun, where the ground is damp. You could use sticks and flat stones to dig. The plastic sheet, weighed down by stones, will trap moist air and cause condensation. If you rest a pebble above your bucket, the condensed water will drip into it.

Page 25 Tepee
10 tent poles • Canvas tarp • Cord
Using the cord, tie together three tent poles, making a tripod. Add the rest of the poles to balance it. Tie your tarp to the top of the roof. Weigh it down with sand or stones.

Page 31 Solar Oven
Aluminum foil • Newspaper
Black construction paper
Pizza box • Craft knife
Plastic wrap
The pizza box, with a flap cut in its lid, forms the oven. Line the base with foil, and cover it with black paper. Pack balled-up newspaper around the edges. Cover the lid with foil, then prop it with a stick. Plastic wrap will seal in the heat.

Page 43 Flashlight
2 D batteries • 2.2 volt light bulb
Electrical tape • Electrical wire
Cardboard tube • Pair of scissors
Tape your batteries so that the negative (-) end of one touches the positive (+) end of the other. Tape the light bulb to the exposed positive end of the batteries. Tape one end of the wire to the exposed negative end of the batteries. Seal one end of the tube with tape. The cardboard tube could be a container for your circuit. Slip your batteries inside, with the wire running through and out of the tube. When the wire touches the metal part of the light bulb, it will glow. This is your on/off switch.

GLOSSARY

absorbing Soaking up.

adapted Changed to better survive an environment.

bacteria Tiny living things that can cause disease.

cairns Piles of stones used to mark a direction.

canyon A narrow valley with steep sides.

condenses Changes from a gas into a liquid.

conserve Prevent waste or loss.

crown The part of a hat that covers the wearer's head.

dehydration A condition caused by extreme loss of water from the body.

disorient Cause to lose a sense of direction.

dunes Mounds of sand.

edible Safe to eat.

evaporating Turning from a liquid into a vapor or gas.

fibers Thin threads of animal, plant, or man-made materials.

friction The force that slows down an object when it is moving against another object or material. Some of the movement turns into heat instead.

hostile Difficult or unfriendly.

impurities Dirt or other unwanted substances.

insulators Materials that prevent heat from going out of, or into, something.

latitudes Measures of the distance north or south of the equator.

linen A hard-wearing fabric woven from the spun fibers of flax.

mammals Group of animals with body hair that feed their young with milk.

navigation Finding your way around.

oasis A place in the desert where water is found.

parasites Living things that live in or on another living thing.

precipitation Rain, snow, or hail that falls to the ground.

rain shadow A region with little rain because it is sheltered by mountains from rain-bearing winds.

seasonal Coming and going at particular times of year.

settlements Villages, towns, or other communities of people.

solar Using the energy of the sun.

SOS The international distress signal.

suffocate To die from a lack of air or from not being able to breathe.

tepee A type of pyramid-shaped tent traditionally used by some Native American peoples.

terminal The metal connection point at the end of a battery.

transpiration Evaporation of water from plants.

ultraviolet light A form of energy from the sun that is not visible to the human eye.

venoms Poisonous substances injected into prey by biting or stinging.

ventilation Movement of fresh air around a closed space.

water vapor Water in the form of a gas.

FURTHER READING

Books

Aloian, Molly. *The Mojave Desert* (Deserts Around the World). St. Catharines, ON: Crabtree, 2012.

Hardyman, Robyn. *Surviving the Desert* (Sole Survivor). New York, NY: Gareth Stevens, 2016.

Levete, Sarah. *Maker Projects for Kids Who Love Exploring the Outdoors* (Be a Maker!). St. Catharines: ON: Crabtree, 2016.

Miles, Justin. *Ultimate Explorer Guide for Kids.* Richmond Hill, ON: Firefly Books, 2015.

Websites

Due to the changing nature of Internet links, PowerKids Press has developed an online list of websites related to the subject of this book. This site is updated regularly. Please use this link to access the list: www.powerkidslinks.com/ms/desert

INDEX

Matthew 6:34
—J.D.

To B.S.
Thank you for encouraging me every day!
Love always
—K.D.

Pete the Cat: Crayons Rock!
Text copyright © 2020 by Kimberly and James Dean
Illustrations copyright © 2020 by James Dean
Pete the Cat is a registered trademark of Pete the Cat, LLC.
All rights reserved. Printed in the United States of America.
No part of this book may be used or reproduced in any manner whatsoever without
written permission except in the case of brief quotations embodied in critical articles and reviews.
For information address HarperCollins Children's Books, a division of HarperCollins Publishers,
195 Broadway, New York, NY 10007.
www.harpercollinschildrens.com
ISBN 978-0-06-286855-8
The artist used pen and ink with watercolor and acrylic paint on
300lb press paper to create the illustrations for this book.
20 21 22 23 24   PC   10 9 8 7 6 5 4 3 2 1
❖
First Edition

Kimberly & James Dean

Pete the Cat

Crayons Rock!

HARPER
An Imprint of HarperCollinsPublishers

Pete loves his big box of groovy crayons!
He loves to draw things like cars, trucks,
flowers, and trees.
And most of all . . . the big blue sea.

From rockin' red
to cool cat blue,
with a box of crayons,
there's nothing
Pete can't do!

One day Pete decided to draw something new . . .

Using lots of colors is so much fun.
Pete wanted to use every one.
He scribbled and drew a great big
smile. His drawings were groovy
and rockin' with style!

Pete was proud of the pictures he drew.
He hoped his friends would dig them, too.

Pete showed Grumpy Toad first.

Grumpy Toad said, "This doesn't look right. Those colors are way too bright."

Pete thought,

"HEY, NO SWEAT. THAT'S ALL RIGHT!"

Pete showed Gus his picture, too.

Gus asked, "Who is this supposed to be? It doesn't really look like me."

Pete thought,

"HEY, NO SWEAT. THAT'S ALL RIGHT!"

Pete finally showed Callie her picture.

Pete said,

"WHAT A

MESS!"

"Bummer. I guess my drawings aren't the best."
Pete started to frown. He put his crayons down.

In art class the teacher asked, "Pete what are you going to make?"
"I don't know—I'm afraid of making a mistake!"

Pete looked around.

Gus drew the coooooolest superheroes.

Callie's flowers were awesome! Out-of-sight!

Grumpy's motorcycle was just right!

Pete's heart sank. His paper was blank.

The gang looked at Pete and said,
"No sweat! It's all right!
"It doesn't have to be just right.

"Your art is cool because it's YOU.
Your art is so unique.

"Grab your groovy box of crayons.
Show us your technique!"

The teacher agreed. "Art should be fun!
Art is for everyone!

"From rockin' red
to cool cat blue,
with a box of crayons,
there's nothing you can't do!"

Pete smiled. "There are no rules. It's no big deal! Art is about how it makes you feel!"

Pete loved his cool art.
That's the one thing Pete knew.
Suddenly, Pete knew *exactly* what to do.

He tried again!

Instead of drawing them one by one,

Pete drew the whole gang, just having fun!

Grumpy Toad, Gus, and Callie agreed
Pete's picture was off the charts!
See? That's the groovy thing about art.